Campaigns are a great training ground to engage in difficult debates, address voters' support, but campaigns also require that one speak forcefully about one's intellectual and emotional capacity to lead. This is new territory for women who have historically been more comfortable being backstage rather in the spotlight. Responding to the prompts in each chapter of the Women Seen and Heard Speaker's Journal *will foster self-awareness and self-confidence, helping women overcome any reticence they might have about asserting their opinions and ideas in public venues. We need more women to have "a place at the table," and when they are elected or appointed, to become a force for social policy changes that will benefit everyone. The political path is not an easy road, and dynamic speaking skills are essential for every woman's success.*

—California State Sen. Hannah-Beth Jackson, D-Santa Barbara

At last, a book that lays out the steps to creating an impactful presentation. In my professional experience, women who are either creating their own family business or family foundation, or who are an aspiring family leader in a family enterprise are finding their voice. As a result, they are wanting more opportunities for top leadership positions. No matter how talented, businesswomen are often struggling with how best to be heard in order to make an impact. That's why this new Speaker's Journal *will certainly provide the tools they wish they had "yesterday." The* Women Seen and Heard Speaker's Journal *provides a pathway to learn how to confidently express their capability and the value they bring to leading their family business into the future.*

—Fran Lotery, PhD, Family Enterprise Consultant, Los Angeles

When it comes to corporate business as of 2018, only 4.8% of Fortune 500 CEOs are women. How can this be? Having vision and intellectual ability are not enough for women to attain high level corporate management positions anywhere near parity with men. CEOs require a particular skill set that include presentation and self-promotion skills and a forceful delivery style, leadership qualities that woman are historically less comfortable with. Specifically, it seems to me that most women are not socialized to be unapologetically competitive. To advance, women need insight into ways to convey strength and command. The Women Seen and Heard Speaker's Journal *gives invaluable insight and many chapters of thoughtful written journal exercises that will provide women with everything they need to attain their leadership goals.*

—Joanna Klein, 20 year TV Development Executive and TV Executive Producer

Dr. Phillips and Dr. Ferguson's book is a timely and valuable resource for women in all fields—whether in politics, public or private sectors. A record number of women won elections across the United States in 2018, making it the so-called 'Year of the Woman.' However, we still see that women have to earn respect and credibility as speakers, and women continue to face a number of complicated dynamics and stereotypes as speakers. The Women Seen and Heard Speaker's Journal *is a clear, concise and strategic guide for women preparing presentations, speeches or testimony. The* WSH Journal *is the resource to assist women in becoming 'the voice of authority' in their presentations.*

—**Kelly Scott, Chief Deputy District Attorney, Santa Barbara County**

Women face many hurdles in the political arena: deciding whether to run, getting their message out as candidates and being heard once in office are among the most difficult. Women often enter politics to effect social justice and propose new public policy. The greatest challenge facing women is being willing to stand up for what we believe in and advocate for our issues. We can do this by developing our own authentic voices. Lois Phillips and Anita Perez Ferguson have written a masterful text that takes you on a trip using self-examination. The Women Seen and Heard Speaker's Journal *provides specific strategies and successful delivery skills that will enable women to use their voices and become more effective leaders. This is a must-read for all women entering the public square.*

—**Hon Susan Rose, Former Board of Supervisors Santa Barbara, California; Founder Santa Barbara Women's Political Committee**

Self-advocacy and eloquence are vital skills for any aspiring woman leader. As a fortunate female leader who has had the firsthand opportunity to be personally coached by Lois Phillips, I can attest that The Women Seen and Heard Speaker's Journal *acts as a straightforward and honest toolkit that can and should inspire women to be both "seen and heard" at their best. Written with the clarity it advocates in its speakers, The* Women Seen and Heard Speaker's Journal *offers timely and versatile advice to every professional woman.*

—**Jennifer Wilson-Buttigieg, Co-Owner & Co-President, Valerie Wilson Travel**

Women Seen and Heard
Speaker's Journal

Women Seen and Heard
Speaker's Journal
WORKBOOK AND TEMPLATES

Lois Phillips, Ph.D. and Anita Perez Ferguson, Ph.D.

Luz Publications

WOMEN SEEN AND HEARD SPEAKER'S JOURNAL
WORKBOOK AND TEMPLATES

by Lois Phillips, Ph.D. and Anita Perez Ferguson, Ph.D.

Printed in the United States of America

Contents

APPENDIX

Introduction:
Lois Phillips & Anita Perez Ferguson

The *Women Seen and Heard Journal* is a companion piece to *Women Seen and Heard: Lessons Learned from Successful Speakers*, published in 2004. In many ways so much has changed in terms of technological advancements, a global economy, and a multicultural society. Yes, women are advancing into managerial positions and more diverse women are entering into political debates, but the number of women in top leadership roles is still disappointing and women have yet to reach a critical mass in numbers that would provide influence. The authors want to see more women enter pathways to economic success and leadership roles across sectors, industries, and fields. We believe that developing a self-confident speaking style is critical for advancing oneself, one's organization, a campaign, or a big idea.

Although we are seeing a positive trend in terms of women's ability to achieve top leadership roles, the numbers are revealing continued inequities. It is true that the 2018 midterm elections began to turn the tide and a historic number of women now serve in the US Congress; however, gender parity remains a goal. One hundred and twenty-seven of four hundred and thirty-five congressional seats, which is under twenty-four percent (or 23.7%) of the Congress, are held by women. Twenty-five (or 25%) of the one hundred senators are women, and one hundred and two women (or 23.4%) of four hundred and thirty-five members of the US House of Representatives are women. Women held about twenty-one percent (or 21.2%) of board seats at Fortune 500 companies in 2018.[1] Three of

---

1   http://www.cawp.rutgers.edu/facts

these boards have zero women directors while there is only one each in pharmaceuticals, the internet sector, and aerospace/defense.[2] Keep in mind that these Boards shape the American economy and media, ensuring that there is accountability and transparency in practices. If women are to advance themselves in top leadership roles across sectors, they need to gain dynamic speaking skills to influence policy development, the allocation of resources, and, in general, how people think and act.

When effective leaders speak to political decision-makers, Board members, and the press, they are able to articulate and often reframe issues in such a way that mobilizes people. This holds true whether women or men are speaking directly to a group, a "live" audience, or meeting "virtually" using teleconferencing media.

The challenges facing women speakers who must communicate with various publics is complicated by the fact that most people are still not used to seeing a woman in a top leadership role. Only 54 women were CEOs of the Fortune 1000 companies. As of March 2017, men made up almost fifty-four percent (or 53.7%) of the federal workforce, but held sixty-six percent (or 66.3 %) of the jobs paying $150,000 or more. Women are half the number of law school entrants but barely thirty-five percent (or 35%) of the women lawyers at law firms make partner. Although women comprise at least forty percent (or 40%) of U.S. medical students, women hold only sixteen (or 16%) of the leadership and executive suite positions such as chief medical officer, chief financial officer, department chair, and dean.

Sex role stereotypes are still prevalent in our culture. Hillary Clinton's failed bid for the presidency was a painful reflection of the implicit bias against women that is still prevalent in our culture. Caroline Heldman, a political scientist at Occidental College who has written about internalized sexism, said in a telephone interview: "We don't like women to be ambitious. It rubs men and women the wrong way."

And when women are assertive, society doesn't necessarily believe them. Journalist Jessica Valenti addressed this when she wrote:

> *"Before the 2016 election, multiple polls showed that voters found Donald Trump more trustworthy than Clinton. Trump's first campaign ad contained one lie every four seconds; and he told at least one lie every day for the first 40 days of his presidency. Yet somehow, still, it was Clinton who couldn't be trusted."*[3]

Sometimes women find themselves in a "double bind" situation. If they don't speak up, they support the status quo. If they do, their speech will be found lacking.[4] Enough members of Congress didn't believe Dr. Christine Blasey Ford's sworn testimony prior to Brett Kavanaugh's appointment to the Supreme Court, where she stated that she was 100% sure that Kavanaugh attacked her during a sexual assault when she was fifteen years old. Dr. Ford's sworn testimony was mocked and derided by the President and his political opponents with few exceptions. Was Dr. Ford mistaken? You simply can't *sort-of* believe her testimony and *sort-of not*, as Senator Susan Collins said in her own way.[5]

We shouldn't be too surprised. When women speak truth to power, their speech is often the subject of mockery based on age-old stereotypes. "Children should be seen and not heard" was a 15th century proverb originally meant for young girls. Starting with sexist comments made by Aristotle and

3 https://www.marieclaire.com/politics/a12825804/believe-women/

4 https://www.catalyst.org/system/files/The_Double_Bind_Dilemma_for_Women_in_Leadership_Damned_if_You_Do_Doomed_if_You_Dont.pdf

5 https://www.motherjones.com/politics/2018/10/susan-collins-brett-kavanaugh-assault-ford/

Plato and other revered philosophers, historians will confirm the power of stereotypes about women's speech, beliefs that women gossip, lie, whine, and are full of guile. As a result, and throughout history, women's complaints were trivialized, their opinions seen as idle chatter. Perhaps this is because men saw women as their intellectual inferiors. As a result, it was commonly thought that women can't get their facts straight and are easily confused, which is just about how Dr. Ford's sworn testimony was described by Kavanaugh's supporters. Never mind that Ford is a proven intellectual with a scholarly track record. And, déjà vu; let's not forget that law professor Anita Hill passed a lie detector test,[6] but her testimony was also dismissed as a pack of lies. Women have a new role model in former UN Ambassador Nikki Haley when the White House dismissed her comments about sanctions on Russia, saying she spoke out of turn. "With all due respect, I don't get confused," she said, showing resilience and grit.

Just because women speakers are prepared and have credentials doesn't mean they'll be believed. Speaking truth to power is a risky business for anyone, but riskier for women than for men. Women speakers are often in a double bind position; that is, women leaders need to be tough-minded to take the heat and navigate skepticism about what they are saying, but, if they are too direct, audiences are turned off, perceiving them abrasive or "masculine." Kristi Hedges writes in Forbes, "… if a woman doesn't show any emotion at all, she can come across as icy and cold. There's a tender balance between emotion and stoicism women must strive for, which men don't have to consider."[7]

Audiences are used to seeing men as the top executives of institutions, corporations, and nonprofit organizations.

---

6   https://www.nytimes.com/2018/09/20/us/politics/anita-hill-testimony-clarence-thomas.html

7   https://www.forbes.com/sites/work-in-progress/2017/03/21/you-talk-like-a-woman-so-what/#6559f19322dc

As a result, audiences are more comfortable accepting a man's voice as the voice of authority. This complicates the dynamics for women speakers. Women CEOs indicated that they "have to integrate the demands of being assertive required by being in a leadership role with being empathetic and transformational in their leadership style." [8]

Just as one builds confidence when one learns to play tennis or ride a bike, practice makes perfect. People gain mastery from making mistakes and from the self-awareness that comes from real-time experiences. One can still feel good about delivering a well prepared, well researched dynamic presentation delivered sincerely, even if the ideas presented are met with skepticism and disbelief. And one never knows whether the ideas presented will ultimately make an impact over time. Anita Hill's consistent, coherent, and sincere testimony ultimately did shift the culture to some degree, and, perhaps Dr. Christine Ford's testimony will have the same effect.

Note that women as a group are effectively using social media to promote themselves, their campaigns, projects, or research. Within three days of her post, Taylor Swift motivated 65,000 young people to register to vote. Having a virtual presence on Facebook is one way to be seen and heard. As of 2018, women were fifty-two percent of Facebook's 2.19 billion users.

Presentations of every type are routinely recorded and found on YouTube. Think about what this means for you. You never know when someone listening to you might record your presentation on their iPhone and post your remarks on Facebook or Instagram, whether you are dressed for success or not. Then, they might decide to Google you and consider supporting your innovative project or product via Crowdfunding.

Not only is social media a fact of life today, women should appreciate the power of social media and how to use social media for good purposes. For example, by using social media, actress Alyssa Milano started a revolution. Women

---

8   https://money.cnn.com/2018/01/31/pf/female-ceos-leadership/index.html

across the world raised their voices in unison to address sexual harassment in the workplace. Starting with producer Harvey Weinstein, their revelations soon extended to harassment experiences across industry, sector, and field. The scandal went viral, and #METOO became an international phenomenon. In spite of the embarrassing and compromising positions they were in, women continued to speak up with candor about their experiences, using every media platform possible. As a result of the outcry, the Motion Picture Academy was forced to take action and immediately stated that "the era of willful ignorance and shameful complicity in sexually predatory behavior and workplace harassment in our industry is over." [9]

As a result of speaking up and telling their stories, many of these women lost their jobs or careers. Still, women interviewed by the press expressed gratitude for the chance to break their silence and the healing that ensued. The reverberations are being felt throughout all industries as part of a cultural revolution. At the time of this writing, corporate firings continue to make headlines.

Social media can raise any of us to prominence on a national or global stage. For instance, we see the power of social media in MJ Hegar's 3.5 minute "Doors" congressional campaign video.[10] Hegar successfully ran for Texas's 31st District seat which had been held by eight-term Republican John Carter. She is a mom and veteran with quite a powerful story to tell. Hegar's campaign video demonstrated how she overcame huge obstacles and setbacks, dramatized her accomplishments, and in doing so, opened new doors for herself and others.

Hegar's message was simple: She believes she can best represent the veterans' predicaments that have been ignored by Congress. Her video ad attracted 1.8 million viewers in the first week it went viral and then, exponentially spread to 4.7 million

9   https://www.washingtonpost.com/.../Oscars-organization-votes-to-expel-disgraced-mogul...

10 Doors campaign video, https://www.youtube.com/watch?v=Zi6v4CYNSI

views via YouTube, appealing to enormous audiences across the country, and quickly out-raising the incumbent. Lesson learned? Whether you take any campaign public-marketing, fundraising, or political campaign- every one of us must consider how we look and how we sound. Have those sound bites at the ready. After all, your well-meaning colleague might record your remarks on her iPhone and decide to share them with domestic colleagues or a global public.

We need to have more women speaking up. The complex dilemmas society faces are of a scale and scope never seen before. We need to harness all the brainpower we can get. Society can only benefit when women are at the table debating current issues. There's a lot to lose if we're not. As the saying goes, "If you're not at the table, you're on the menu." [11] The controversial issues of the day affect women's status and circumstances in unique ways. These include access to affordable quality child care, housing, student debt, job inequality and pay inequity, equal opportunities, fair representation in the media, domestic violence, untested rape kits, reproductive choice, sexual harassment and bullying, and the lack of an Equal Rights Amendment.

Debating today's controversial issues will inevitably cause tensions and conflicts will escalate. It's easy to throw up one's hands and walk away. But women speakers who have developed speaking skills (and the resulting self-confidence) will remain tenacious, even through difficult debates with personal attacks. As a group, women cross racial, ethnic, and cultural boundaries. When diverse women find common ground and express their ideas and opinions for addressing social ills, everyone will benefit including boys and men.

---

11 "…on the menu." This quote is believed to have originated around 2000 in Washington, DC, and is of unknown origin. Basically, it means that if you are not represented at the decision-making table, you are in a financially vulnerable position, you get left out, or, worse yet, you are on the menu (overcooked, sliced up, and devoured).

The premise of our 2004 book, *Women Seen and Heard: Lessons Learned from Successful Speakers* remains true even today. Women speakers need to be twice as good as men are when they deliver presentations, even if they are competent, have demonstrated the expertise appropriate for the topic, and have legitimate authority in a particular role.[12] Men have always been in top leadership roles and the public is used to hearing men speak with authority, so men start with credibility when they begin their remarks. On the other hand, women have to earn it. Sure, to hold listeners' attention, they have to be effective communicators but, unlike men, who start their presentations with the benefit of the doubt, women speakers still need to gain credibility as "the voice of authority" before anyone will pay attention to their message.

What's the point? If you're reading this book, you want to overcome any reticence you might have about being or becoming a more dynamic speaker. There are ways to prepare more strategically for your presentations than suggestions given in textbooks. First, because stereotypes persist, women speakers must clarify the reasons the listeners need to trust them. *Ask yourself, what special expertise do I bring to the table? What's my track record? What can I do for them (my team, this group, the audience, or the listeners)?*

Second, establish the desired end game of a presentation before putting ideas to paper. Clarify for yourself: *What's the main point of my talk? What do I want to leave people with? What do I want listeners to do? What steps do I want them to take?*

Third, to drive home your main point, choose the most relevant article ("ripped from the headlines") or a few examples that will be fascinating and fresh. Ask yourself: *What great stories can I share from history or real life that will engage people emotionally and support my main point?*

---

12 https://money.cnn.com/2018/01/31/pf/female-ceos-leadership/index.html

Women are socialized to connect. That's an advantage as you continue to improve your speaking skills. You may want to sound conversational as if the ideas were simply rolling off your tongue without preparation but let's agree: speaking to an audience is *not* a conversation. And let's face it, some women can meander, disclose self-doubts, and use a "spiral logic" to eventually get to the point (if there is a point). That may work with your BFF but it doesn't work well in a presentation, even to an all-women's group. In fact, women are tougher critics of women speakers than men are.

To ensure that your audience knows that you do have a point to make, you need to be strategic and be particularly well-organized. Start with an overarching single "Key Message Point," stated in one simple sentence. Have clarity and leave nothing to chance. Without clarity, your speech could be a muddle of disparate ideas.

Of course you want to connect and have your listeners like you but something needs to happen as a result of a presentation. That "something" could be having the audience understand something that had been complicated, helping your listeners experience a "click" or have a "eureka" moment! If you are going to persuade people to do something, you must articulate a "call to action," ideally one that has your audience reaching for their checkbook, cheering, or endorsing your big idea. If you're going to inspire your listeners, you may want them to smile and nod or even experience a teary moment. Unlike casual conversations, a polished presentation requires planning ahead. There's nothing magical about it.

What bugs you? The prompts in the "Speaker's Journal" will encourage you to think about your values, ideas, opinions, and the issues you care about most. As a result of your notations, the journal entries will clarify how you're feeling about a topic and move you along in being able to speak about it. Between life and work, family and friends, volunteering and hobbies, you have fascinating experiences you've learned from, experiences you can utilize to make a point through story telling.

Everything you jot down in the journal will increase your ability to provide ideas for what you want to say to others. Start small, sharing your ideas with your friends and family. Then move on to trusting co-workers. You'll gather momentum and gain clarity each time you explain your ideas and opinions to others. Expressing your ideas out loud will help you clarify where you need further explanations or better transitions between your various points.

Some presentations are simply updates or briefings but other presentations have more at stake. Presenting yourself effectively means getting that job or promotion, gaining funding for a project, finding clients, or getting elected. Using the "Speaker's Journal" will provoke you to do some soul searching. You'll think back to the conditions that affected your attitude towards speaking up. You'll recall the times you did so well and were on *a natural high* after an interview, a team meeting, or a more formal presentation.

Know thyself. There are psychological blocks that cause speaker reticence. You might question your own capacity for wisdom and ask yourself, "Who am I to tell people how to think or what to do?" All of us have innate strengths. Feedback about one's strengths (and limitations) coming from a respected and more experienced mentor can help individuals blossom. Role models show us what a polished speaker looks like and sounds like. Mentors help people build on their innate strengths and experiences. Sponsors are known to open doors for talented employees, helping them stretch and overcome any speaking anxiety they might have. One coach provided an opportunity for a reticent speaker to participate in a panel discussion. Another coach asked his protégée to lead a team meeting. All of these small steps forward build a speaker's confidence and there are "lessons learned" from each speaking transaction.

Alas, not everyone has had positive role models or mentors who encouraged them to express their ideas and feelings in group settings. The journaling process allows every woman to gain self-confidence through self-reflection. Responding to the prompts we provide can be therapeutic with regard to the reasons why a person had been reticent to speak up. Journaling also provides a chance to clarify one's values and articulate those "big ideas." A journal is private, writing can be therapeutic, and themes that emerge provide a chance to see patterns in one's life that might otherwise be apparent. Journals give us clarity about ourselves so that we can say to others, "I deeply value…[13]" or "I've traveled extensively so I appreciate the creativity found in a multi-cultural workplace."

The Speaker's Journal also lists helpful websites that provide motivational quotes and blogs about women speakers. The resources will be useful material to incorporate into your presentations. If you're looking for role models, you'll find a list of web links to examples of real speeches by dynamic presenters in your field, sector, or industry. Search Google for people you admire and find presentations delivered at professional conferences to learn what made them successful. Google TED.com and find the topics that interest you. You'll find international speakers to inspire you. They may make delivering a presentation look easy but keep in mind that these speakers are professionally coached and well-rehearsed.

We want to make life easy for you! Everyone is busy these days and few people have speaking coaches helping them prepare. Knowing that, consider the nine "Speaker Templates" as "cheat sheets." The Templates will ensure that your presentations are easy to follow with room for embellishment.

The audience will find it easy to follow your train of thought if every presentation—whether a briefing or a pitch presentation—contains a structure that flows. That's why every Template we provide ensures you will have an Introduction,

---

13 For example, "I deeply value the power of community."

Body, and Conclusion and reminders about expanding upon your points with examples and data.

The Templates are worksheets. Think of them as skeletal outlines, which make it easy to input your own content. The Templates provide a structure to organize your flow of ideas and examples. They guarantee there will be a logical flow of points and/or an emotional build-up, all the better to ensure you will engage your listeners. Each one can be modified to meet your needs. Some Templates have content provided.

Each Template provides space for you to elaborate upon your "Key Message Point" and ensure that you include explanatory sub-points. And they won't squelch your creativity. You'll supply the engaging anecdotes, quotes, statistics, visual aids, demonstrations, and personal stories to flesh out your main point and make the topic come to life.

Even if you're passionate about your subject matter, the Templates will force you to be disciplined about how you present your ideas. Women, in particular, must control their passion for the subject matter so that it is always offered in service of their main idea.

Finally, the range of Templates will help you save time. They include types of presentations that are typically required for work or optional presentations one delivers at a social occasion. They include:

1. The Informative Presentation
2. The Persuasive Presentation
3. The Inspirational Presentation
4. The Persuasive Presentation to Pitch a New Product or Service
5. The Call to Action Presentation
6. The Campaign Pitch
7. The Humorous Presentation
8. The "Small Wins" Informative Presentation
9. Delivering a Toast to the Bride and Groom

If you use the Templates, you'll more likely be successful when you provide a purposeful briefing, move your listeners to action, inspire people to succeed, toast the happy couple, and tickle the funny bone.

Our country needs to hear from more women leaders in every sector and field who can think creatively about how to connect diverse people by finding common ground. Creating common ground with an audience is like clearing a pathway from their heart to yours.[14] Dynamic speakers can do just that, and women have the capacity to be dynamic speakers. After all, women are known to excel at connecting people and connecting with people. In today's fast paced, multicultural society and high tech environment, the old military and economic paradigms aren't working and we need to hear from more diverse women in making decisions that will shape the future. As global strategist Parag Khanna writes,

> "We're accelerating into a future shaped less by countries than by connectivity. (Hu)Mankind has a new maxim—Connectivity is destiny— and the most connected powers, and people, will win.[15]

When you're tempted to confide in a friend that you're nervous about a presentation, substitute the word "excited." Excitement is a good thing. After all, we all want that adrenalin rush to provide the energy we need to stay focused and connected. As society charts its future, we need to hear from more (and more diverse) women's voices. May your voice be one of them!

---

14 https://www.duarte.com/great-presentations-create-common-ground/

15 Connectography: Mapping the Future of Global Civilization, Parag Khanna, also a CNN Global Contributor

SECTION ONE

Women Seen and Heard
Journal

SECTION ONE

SPEAKER'S JOURNAL

The prompts provided in the "Speaker's Journal" section are based on the content of *Women Seen and Heard: Lessons Learned from Successful Speakers* (2004). Please respond to the prompts as you read through each chapter of the *Speaker's Journal*. You'll want to use a spiral bound notebook to write your responses to the questions we pose.

Even if you haven't read *Women Seen and Heard*, these prompts have a logical flow to them and each chapter in the "Speaker's Journal" builds on the prompts that appear in the one before it. Most important, your responses will lead you to refine your ideas, clarify your values, and remember experiences that can be polished and incorporated into future presentations or formal speeches.

CHAPTER 1

Women Seen and Heard Speaker's Journal

Asserting Your Leadership Through Public Speaking

"Communication is the real work of leadership."
—Nitin Nohria, Harvard Business School
professor and author of *Beyond The Hype*

1. How do you feel about public speaking? Describe the feelings you have: pride, excitement, or anxiety? Why do you think you feel this way?

2. Do you believe that women have a different point of view than men do about how society is structured? How do you and the men in your life differ in terms of your points of view about life?

3. Did you ever speak up about an issue that was controversial? Did asserting yourself help you to connect with people? If not, describe the negative reaction or fallout.

4. Have you ever been in a workplace or political or academic meeting in which you were the only woman in the group? If so, what feelings did you have about being in that situation?

5. Given the above, you must have had an opinion about a topic under discussion. How did you establish your

expertise when you expressed your opinion? Describe the dynamics and what happened.

6. What would you do differently in a similar speaking situation next time, if anything?

7. Leaders affect changes in how people think, feel, and behave. Are you willing to become a leader in your community, workplace, or professional association? What would it take for you to step up and put yourself out front?

8. Select an issue of the day that concerns you. Do you have an opinion on what could change for the better? What needs to change?

9. Does this issue affect you personally? Did this issue have an impact on you or your family or a friend? What is needed to lead a change for the better?

10. What would friends expect you to say about this issue? Would you surprise them?

11. Are you willing to become a voice for change and speak up about this particular issue, thus becoming known as a leader (or ringleader) in your community, workplace, or professional association? What are the pros and cons of speaking up?

12. Identify one or two issues affecting women that you care about but that are being overlooked by existing leaders of groups, organizations, associations, companies and agencies or appointed or elected officials. These could be (but not limited to) such issues as the need for affordable child care, safety in schools or our streets, housing, opportunities for advancement, or the high cost of health care. Explain why you think that these issues are being overlooked.

13. What would your main point be if you were delivering a presentation about an issue that you care about? State it in one sentence.

14. Leaders have access to resources and can make things happen. What would your top three priorities be if you were in charge of a group, company, agency, school, etc.?

CHAPTER 2

Women Seen and Heard Speaker's Journal

Women Speakers Face Unique Challenges

"You must do the thing you think you cannot do."
—Eleanor Roosevelt, Progressive Activist,
Advocate and Outspoken First Lady

1. Our family members play an enormous role in shaping our identity. Did your parent(s)/family raise you to be a homemaker and to excel in that role, or did they encourage you to seek a full-time career? Explain the impact of their encouragement on you as you matured.

2. How did these early experiences affect your desire to speak up in your classes, join the school council, or lead a team?

3. How did women in your family play leadership roles when decisions had to be made? Did they argue? Did they cajole others?

4. Did you excel in a particular field, sport, or skill? Did you experience a "natural high" and "adrenalin rush" from having people watch you perform?

5. How has your early family life prepared you to be a leader? Did your mother and/or father or other relatives believe that you would be a leader? Did they encourage you to be a "good girl" and not make waves?

6. Speakers need to be comfortable standing in their own light. Our sex-role socialization can prepare girls to be modest and not prideful. What was the message you received about girls bragging about good grades, musical /artistic prowess, appearance, or athletic performance? How did this affect you psychologically?

7. Describe a situation in which you held back your true feelings and instead, you "bit your tongue?" What were the risks of speaking out? If there had been no fear, what would you have said?

8. Selecting a "woman's issue" from the list of typical "women's issues," why do you relate to this issue as a daughter, parent, professional, employer, activist, or advocate?

9. Have you ever had the power to lead an effort to improve a situation because of 1) your expertise, 2) your personal networks, 3) personal charisma, wit, or charm, or 4) your financial or organizational resources? Describe what happened. How did that feel?

10. Think about a time when you had to assert yourself in dealing with another person with whom you have a personal or collegial relationship. What made you speak up? Explain how you felt afterwards.

11. What did you learn from asserting yourself in a one-to-one conversation that can be applied to asserting yourself (your opinions and ideas) in front of an audience?

12. Girls are encouraged to have a pleasant soothing speaking voice. What have you noticed about the difference between men and women's voices when you listen to public speakers? Consider body language, tone of voice, story-telling skills, how they organize ideas, etc.

13. Sometimes women sound like girls, even when middle aged. Record yourself reading a paragraph from a book or the newspaper. Is it a high pitched voice? Is it a "sing song" style? What message are you sending by the way you sound?

14. Tentative women won't influence listeners. End your sentences with an upward or rising inflection and your statements will sound like questions (also called a "Valley Girl" style). Do you have "vocal fry," a style marked by a low, slightly creaky sound at the end of sentences?" [16]

---

16 For a demonstration, watch it here: https://www.youtube.com/watch?v =UsE5mysfZsY

CHAPTER 3

Women Seen and Heard Speaker's Journal

Role Models Are Important

"I tell my daughters to have their voice in this world, and it became clear I needed to role-model that."
—Melinda Gates, the world's most powerful advocate for women and girls and co-founder The Bill & Melinda Gates Foundation

1. What are your feelings about the women in history or women you read about who spoke up? If you're not sure, use the Internet for access to biographies and select one accomplished woman. How does her biography and back-story relate to you, if at all?

2. Who are the other women in your workplace or your family who are watching you and listening to your ideas and opinions (e.g., sisters, daughters, cousins)? Who might see you as a "role model," or mentor?

3. Describe anyone—teacher, boss, colleague, or family member—who was a "mentor" for you, someone who took you under her or his wing and encouraged you to develop your talents. How did you benefit from his or her advice? Explain whether his or her advice helped you become a better listener or speaker.

4. When you think of outstanding women speakers, whose name or face comes to mind? List 3–5.

5. What is there about any of these women (i.e., her behavior, image, or attitude) that makes you believe she is or could be a leader? Is it her poise, presence, self-confidence, liveliness, and/or ability to be articulate? Is it another characteristic? Describe specific behaviors wherever possible.

6. Considering an outstanding woman speaker, how are you and "the outstanding speaker" alike? How are you different?

7. Think of a time when you broke new ground and were "the first woman" (e.g., bank president, brain surgeon, PTA President, litigator, team captain, etc.) in a particular role. How did you feel? Were you self-conscious? Were you dismissive of the status you held? Did you make light of your advancement? How did you handle it?

8. Think about a particular accomplishment that you're proud of. When might you refer to this accomplishment in a presentation in a way that would be relevant? Explain whether you typically refer to or ignore your prior accomplishments when you speak to groups. What accomplishment might you brag about in public?

9. When you do speak in public, in what situations are you most self-confident? In what situations are you least self-confident, more awkward and more self-conscious? What's different about these two types of situations?

10. Describe your style as a speaker: Are you direct or indirect? Do you have strong opinions? How do you handle conflict? Do you avoid conflict or deal with it in a straightforward way?

11. Sometimes the listeners are going to be resistant to a change you propose. When do you find yourself softening

your hard-hitting points so as not to offend? How effective is that?

12. In one simple sentence, state one, two or three proposals you might make to a team, group, company, best friends, or...your family! Start with "I propose that we..." or "I suggest that we..."

13. A woman's image is important because it is part of her "meta-message." How would other people describe you in terms of your appearance?

14. Are you fashion-conscious or fashion-averse? Do you consider your appearance when you're going to be in a business or political situation? What statement do you want to make by your appearance?

15. Women in leadership roles are scrutinized more critically by women as well as by men. (See research below.[17]) Have you ever felt unfairly scrutinized when you expressed an opinion or felt socially isolated when you were in a management or leadership role? If so, explain how you handled it and any lessons learned.

> 'In male-dominated societies women often cannot be both liked and perceived as competent at the same time. "We call this the double bind." Take Hilary Clinton for example—the more she had "gravitas" the less likable she was to many men (and women), yet when she showed a more feminine side, her "stamina" was brought into question.'

16. Think of Anita Hill and Dr. Christine Blasey Ford speaking against the candidates nominated to the Supreme

---

17 https://www.managementtoday.co.uk/give-women-leaders-hard-time/women-in-business/article/1420560

Court, Clarence Thomas and Brett Kavanaugh respectively. Their sworn testimony was found lacking. After speaking your mind to a skeptical group, would you be tough enough to deal with rejection? Explain why (or whether) you believe you'd have the strength or resilience to "speak truth to power."

CHAPTER 4

Women Seen and Heard Speaker's Journal

Feminine Traits Are Human Traits

**"In politics, if you want anything said, ask a man.
If you want anything done, ask a woman."**
　　　—Margaret Thatcher, Britain's first female
　　　prime minister

*According to research, feminine traits include being cooperative,
communicative, soft-spoken, modest, process-oriented, relation-
al, and with the ability to readily express emotions. Masculine
traits include competitiveness, aggressiveness, physical strength,
and an orientation towards goals or action.*

1. How would you describe yourself, using the terms
   "feminine" and "masculine" or "androgynous?" The
   latter term, simply put, is a combination of feminine and
   masculine traits. Describe yourself in a few sentences in
   terms of the traits you use when you communicate with
   people. Include your family, co-workers, and friends and
   give concrete examples of how you behave similarly or
   differently with each.

2. Feminine traits are not usually associated with power.
   This can be a problem for a "feminine" person because
   public speaking requires that the speaker behave in a
   masculine way, controlling the speaking situation and
   dominating the occasion. Feminine traits might create
   additional anxiety for a woman if the speaker's role
   requires her to dominate the occasion or "own the room."

How does your "femininity" or "masculinity" affect your attitude towards speaking to groups, even informally?

3. When women speak to a group, research indicates that most or many women tend to want to relate to their audience more than they want to force their message upon them. Is this true of you?

4. Describe an occasion when the relationship aspect is going to be as important or more important than what you will say.

5. Think of an issue that's on your mind right now. Would you be willing to speak up and fight for a change? *(For example only: Is it lobbying the council for streetlights needed for safety in your neighborhood? Rectifying the favoritism in your department or nepotism in your company? Diversifying the management team? Addressing a bullying problem at your school?)* Select any issue that concerns you, and state your proposal in one sentence starting with "We should..."

6. Using the issue above, state briefly what the benefits would be to others from the change you are proposing.

7. How would you describe your ability to hold your position on a controversial issue and deal with critical feedback, even if it made you unpopular? Would you have the self-confidence to remain tenacious?

8. How can you tell that the audience understands your main message? How can you ensure that the listeners will quote you in the morning?

9. Describe your strengths when you conduct a conversation with someone else. Do you initiate a conversation easily? Do you listen intently? Do you ask good questions? Do you make the other person feel that you can relate to what

he or she is saying? Can you pay attention and remain focused?

10. Describe situations in which you have had to get up and speak "off the cuff." Was that easier or more difficult than a more formal presentation? What made it different?

11. If you have particular expertise, how do you convey your confidence in your competence?

12. Do you feel confident when you present accurate and current facts and figures? Do you feel self-confident because you have street smarts from years of life experience? Have you gained self-confidence from years of completing complicated projects at work?

13. Women like to connect. Think of one great personal story you might tell about your background or overcoming great odds, a story that would allow people to connect to you and trust you.

CHAPTER 5

Dynamic Speakers Are Authentic: Know Yourself, Be Yourself

"We have to dare to be ourselves, however frightening or strange that self may prove to be."
—May Sarton, novelist, poet, memoirist, and strong individualist

1. After they hear your remarks, what aspect of your life do you want your audience(s) to understand and appreciate?

2. Sometimes we are forced to attend a formal or public event. How do you prepare to "be yourself?" What do you think about (or worry about) beforehand, if anything?

3. How eager are you to be "seen?" Describe your state of mind and eagerness to be social.

4. How well do you know yourself? What is most important to you? Explain what it is that you value, prize and cherish the most.

5. It's easy to be caught up in our roles, routines and responsibilities and not think about a legacy. What do you want to achieve in your lifetime?

6. What really ticks you off? What or who can push your buttons and make you snap? Describe situations that might find you feeling this way.

7. After you present a report at a meeting there are typically questions. How might you handle a confrontation during the Q and A? Some people are cool under pressure but how well do you/can you manage difficult questions or difficult people? Give an example and explain.

8. Describe any important life experiences or key relationships that have led you to your particular core beliefs and core values about what's most important in life. Besides the people in your life, consider your travels, spiritual/religious experiences, or cross-cultural experiences.

9. Why have you (or haven't you) shared your values in public with coworkers, friends and family members?

10. Some speakers are powerful and can be influential in changing minds and hearts. Was there a speaker you've heard who convinced you to change your mind about a problem or particular situation, and to see things from his or her point of view? What was it about their delivery style or framework that affected you the most?

11. It can be risky to share too much about your private circumstances, failures, missteps, or limitations. On the other hand, self-disclosure could be a way to connect more deeply with people.[18] Given the topics you want to (or already) speak about, what personal information would be appropriate to share with a group? Describe the potential risks and/or the positive benefits of appropriate self-disclosure.

12. You're unique. What might be interesting about you that few people know? Consider the places you've traveled to, weird or amusing living arrangements, building your

---

18 In 2004, Apple CEO Steve Jobs told his workers that he was seriously ill. The news had emotional and financial repercussions. In 2010 country singer Glen Campbell told audiences that he was diagnosed with Alzheimer's disease.

own home, raising a foster child, raising money for a good cause, being a fashionista or tutoring an immigrant. Give three specific examples. Will you share them tomorrow with friends or your family?

13. There are always some topics that we would die on our sword to defend. On what topic might people perceive you as being inflexible, abrasive or "having an edge?" And, how do you feel about that?

14. Good speakers consider that the listeners might have values, beliefs, goals, and needs different from their own. Think about delivering a presentation to a group of people who are very different from you. How you can relate *your key message* to this particular group or audience so they appreciate your expertise and point of view? What would you do?

15. Select a specific subject you might actually speak about to a group of friends or colleagues. Engaging speakers often use humor or fictitious characters from novels, TV shows, or films to introduce their topic, even when their main point is serious. Which comedic or fictional character from a novel or film might you refer to in your opening remarks as a bridge to your main point? Think of Atticus Finch, Luke Skywalker, Lois Lane, or Hawkeye.[19]

16. We need to convey that we understand our listeners and share common dilemmas. What are some frustrating or challenging situations of our busy lives that are common

---

19 https://www.listchallenges.com/famous-fictional-characters-everyone-knows

to men or women? Select an everyday example that anyone could relate to.[20]

17. We all love people who don't take themselves too seriously and are able to gently poke fun at their own failings but women tend to overdo self-disclosure anecdotes, which can backfire. What humorous stories might you be tempted to share about your foibles that might actually do more harm than good and undermine your credibility as an expert or as a leader?

18. Identify one issue that you think is important but that is being overlooked by the existing leadership. Explain why you care about this issue, and what might happen if this issue isn't resolved. Why should other people care about this issue? What's in it for them?

19. Do you have a "fresh take" on a controversial issue? Explain what that is and why *you* do.

20. What are the risks of speaking up about this or any other controversial issue? What's to be gained? What could be lost?

21. Think about a work, social, political, or family group to which you belong. Name the group. What bugs you about this group? If you were in charge of the group, what would your top three priority goals be? List three, starting with number one.

22. In pitching your idea for one positive change, what would you argue that the benefits would be? List the benefits!

---

20 Examples of common dilemmas: We lose our keys because we are juggling too many roles. We can forget an appointment or forget to put gas in the tank. We have an aging parent living far away. We live beyond our means. We get addicted to cable news. Keeping up with the competition is exhausting.

Early Influences Shape Our Attitudes About Speaking Up

> "Life always gives us exactly the teacher we need at every moment. This includes every mosquito, every misfortune, every red light, every traffic jam, every obnoxious supervisor (or employee), every illness, every loss, every moment of joy or depression, every addiction, every piece of garbage, every breath. Every moment is the guru."
> —Charlotte Joko Beck, Zen Teacher and Author

1. In general, parents can shape our attitudes towards communication. Briefly describe what you recall about dinner table conversations or family reunions. Did you enjoy hearing people express their ideas, opinions, or share anecdotes about family history? How did that affect you in developing your own communication style, if at all?

2. Were there repercussions when family members spoke their minds? What did you learn about how to communicate from the women in your family?

3. Growing up, the relationships you had with family members shaped you and helped you develop attitudes about communication with others. Was it okay to debate issues and express different opinions?

4. What values and attitudes did you gain from your family? List as many as you can. How did those values and attitudes affect who you became in your adult life? [21]

5. Were your parents or family members involved in church, community or charitable groups as volunteers? Were they involved in local politics? If not, did they mistrust such groups and keep their opinions to themselves? What did you learn about communication from watching them engage with others?

6. Did your parents have expectations for you to perform well in school? How did their expectations affect you?

7. Were you active in extracurricular activities and clubs that required you to communicate with others? Were you in a leadership role in any club? Were you in a drama or debate club? If not, why not? If so, how did these experiences affect you in terms of developing your communication style?

8. Did your parents or family members read articles, journals, or classical literature? Did you gain an appreciation for eloquent written or spoken language from them, from your education, or personal pursuits? How did this affect you as an adult when it came to your writing or speaking style?

9. Did your parents or family members advocate for what they believed to be right through volunteerism or through political advocacy? What social risks did they take, if any? If they did speak up for their beliefs, what did you learn from them about the importance of *walking-the-talk*?

---

21 These values might include integrity, frugality, common courtesy, love of nature, cleanliness, fairness, love of learning, a mistrust of authority or government, discipline, morality, religious or spiritual values, etc.

10. Did you speak up in your school classes and debate issues? Were you in student council? Did you resist involvement, seeing yourself as less capable than your peers who were school leaders? How comfortable are you debating issues, even now? Do you take it personally if people don't agree with you?

11. Describe yourself as a young child through your High School years in terms of your size, height, weight, etc. Were you "average" or outstanding in some way? How would your peers have described you?

12. Explain whether you developed a positive or self-critical image of yourself from your childhood, an image that lasted and affected your adult years. Did you blossom and evolve as you matured?

13. Did you have a mentor from college or a work situation, someone who believed in you? If so, explain the value of his or her mentoring you received, or explain how the lack of a mentor might have affected your self-confidence as a speaker.

14. Did you have a work role that required you to give orders, such as "Just Do It!" or "March!" or "Strike!" How comfortable was that role for you?

15. Did you have experience teaching or training others in a skill? What do you imagine is the value of a teaching or training role in helping you or any person develop speaking skills?

When Planning Your Presentation, Have a Strategy in Mind

"How you act (gravitas), how you speak (communication), and how you look (appearance) count for a lot in determining your leadership presence."

—Sylvia Hewitt, Economist

1. When it's an issue that a woman speaker cares deeply about, she tends to make a persuasive pitch from a heart-centered approach. If the speaker is sincere and provides facts and figures, she will assume people will want to believe her. Alas, just because *you* care about something doesn't mean your listeners will. Give an example of a presentation you made in which you spoke from the heart. What worked and what didn't? What might you do differently?

2. Given stereotypes about women's emotionality, women speakers need to ensure that their arguments are sound and logical with a balanced amount of emotional appeal. They need to make their case strategically, in ways that will win over even the most skeptical person. As practice, choose an issue that you care about and consider the evidence you might give to make your case.

3. Think of a position you hold. To convince people to align with this particular position, explain how you would get their attention. Choose a shocking headline, a visual aid or heartwarming example, choose a quote from an esteemed expert, or the latest, hot statistics.

4. To persuade an audience to do something new or change a plan of action, you will need to persuade listeners that your plan has particular benefits to them, more so than what they are presently doing or avoiding doing. Think of one change that would improve your community and simply state it in one sentence. State it as "I propose..." and finish the sentence. Provide a few benefits of your proposal.[22]

5. Some people are visual thinkers. Words and numbers won't move them off the dime, nor will PowerPoint slides displaying poorly conceived pie charts or black and white excel spread sheets with tiny fonts. What visuals would help your audience appreciate the change you are proposing? Explain how you would use visuals to make the main point of a particular presentation come alive.[23]

6. Women have a tendency to be indirect and ambiguous, particularly when they are asking for something for themselves to include a campaign contribution, an endorsement, or a promotion.[24] What do you want from your listeners? Don't leave them wondering what you

---

22 Examples might include: On-site affordable child care, more bus routes, affordable housing, more after-school programs in music and drama, diversifying the City Council, safer streets, etc.

23 Examples might include: 1) Stunning photos, 2) BEFORE and AFTER photos that display changes, 3) An animation versus a still photo, 4) A demonstration of how to do or make something.

24 *The Power of Talk: Who Gets Heard and Why,* Deborah Tannen, Harvard Business Review, September–October 1995 Issue

are asking of them. Briefly state a proposal you will or might make to a particular team or group in simple, clear language.[25]

7. Speakers with a big idea have to convey self-confidence. How will you convey that you are personally very confident about the brilliance of your big idea?

8. What might you do to prepare to pitch your big idea to decision-makers? Do you need to do some networking, dive into more research, prepare great visuals, or hobnob with donors or investors?

9. List the ways in which you are a legitimate expert on a subject you care about. Include your community involvement, studies, work, travel, academic knowledge, publications, awards, honors, and any other accomplishments.[26]

10. Stereotypes convey that women are more emotional than men and less strategic. Your listeners need to know that you aren't easily manipulated by your feelings and can stay the course. What examples can you give of times you made a tough decision? When did you remain tenacious, cool, and strong in the midst of a crisis? When did you turn around a lost cause and save a sinking ship?

---

25 Examples: We need to start charging members higher dues. We need to enforce the rules of meeting Start/End times. I need your vote. I'm asking you to volunteer five hours a week to my campaign.

26 Examples of conveying your expertise: "I've spent two years working in the field with...and have learned five lessons that saved hundreds of lives."

CHAPTER 8

Women Seen and Heard Speaker's Journal

Flawless Delivery

"We need women at all levels, including the top, to change the dynamic, reshape the conversation, to make sure women's voices are heard and heeded, not overlooked and ignored."

—Sheryl Sandberg

1. A flawless presentation means a successful presentation that affects the listeners. Not one thing needs to be changed. Based on your standards and criteria for excellence, how do you define "flawless?" Who else might determine whether your presentation is or isn't "flawless?"

2. A persuasive presenter might want votes, dollars, empowerment, or tears. What is your criteria for success, given your desire to be persuasive about a particular issue?

3. What could you do to relax and focus before your presentation?

4. What have you learned about your speaking style from prior presentations that you want to change, do more of, do less of, or simply do differently?

5. What can you say to your audience to convey that you really do want to be delivering this (or any) presentation?

6. Have you listened to yourself on tape? Is your voice easy to listen to? Do you emphasize your key points with

variety in volume, pitch, and rate of speech? Do you tend to use upward inflections at the end of the sentences?

7. Listen to a few women who are broadcast anchors and compare your voice and speaking style to theirs. Avoid upward inflections or guttural growl ("vocal fry"). Leave a voice mail message for yourself and listen to your tone, rate of speaking and pitch. What might you want to change?

8. When you stand up to speak to a group, you have thirty seconds to get out of the gate and hit the ground running. Think of a topic that interests you. How can (or will) you get the audience's attention? How will you gain their trust as someone with expertise?

9. Presentations can be humorous, technical, personal, and/ or rely on PowerPoint slides and other media. Select a topic you enjoy or might need to address and think about how many different ways you could present this topic to engage your audience? [27]

10. Speakers often don't think about their *purpose* before they organize their thoughts. Your purpose might be to inform, persuade, motivate, inspire, entertain or acknowledge a special occasion. What was the purpose of a recent (upcoming, or possible) presentation? Explain the context and why your purpose was appropriate.

11. Think of a brief presentation you have given. What did you learn from that one? With the wisdom of hindsight, what would you have done more of or less of?

12. Then, consider taking that same briefing and elaborating on the subject in a longer presentation on the same topic delivered to a more formal audience (perhaps to include

---

27 See all Templates in Section II including the HUMOR Template.

top executives, a board, investors, donors, or a public body). What specific changes to your remarks might you make as you adapt it to this?

13. How might you solicit feedback after any presentation about how well you delivered your ideas? Regarding your delivery style, what specific feedback would you want?

CHAPTER 9

Women Seen and Heard Speaker's Journal

Storytelling and Relating

"There's always room for a story that can transport people to another place."
—J.K. Rowling, Novelist, Philanthropist,
Screenwriter and Producer

1. A story has a beginning, middle, and end. It includes who, what, when, where, and why. But some presenters stick to hard data and only the facts. What is the value of using stories to engage your audience?

2. Using a dramatic story to liven up your presentation is known to work well but it must align with your topic. Select a topic and then think of a personal story that you might share that would be "on point." [28] Make sure the story won't have you in tears or giggles as you tell it!

3. Give an example of a personal story or situation that changed your life. What topic might it relate to? For instance, it might involve a life-changing trip, a health crisis, a mentor's advice, a film or novel that changed your life, or an historic moment that led to adopting political or religious beliefs. Then, articulate in one simple sentence the point or the moral of this particular story.

---

28   Your story should have: 1) an emotional hook that would gain the listeners' attention, 2) characters who do things *and* have feelings or ideas, 3) a summary of what happened or "the plot," 4) a conflict between people or groups, and 5) a resolution of the conflict.

4. When sharing a personal story to make a point, would you consider providing background information about your race, culture, religion, age, ability, special needs, or sexual orientation? Might it be risky or engaging your listeners more deeply? How do you decide?

5. People remember what was said when the statement packs an emotional punch. Putting appropriate emotion into a story can galvanize an audience; for instance, stating the flu season statistics could be boring unless you describe how you recently felt when you contracted the flu. Give an example of a dramatic personal story you could share with a group that would bring statistics to life.

6. How you open and close a presentation is critical to your success. To practice, select a topic you actually might address and state the particular group or audience you might be speaking to. Consider what you already know about your audience (e.g., their demographics, needs, values, and educational level). To hook them, select a provocative headline, choose a quote from a respected scientist, or mention the theme of a beloved film, novel, or TV series.

7. Think of a revealing story that you told someone about yourself and it came back to you later as something they remembered. They may have even quoted you later to other friends. Did the person remember the story because of the content and specific details or the way you told it?

8. Ellen DeGeneres and Sheryl Sandberg are seen as excellent storytellers. Think of someone you know who is an excellent storyteller whose stories you remember. Why do you remember their stories? Be specific. Again, is it the fascinating content of the stories they tell or their delivery style?

9. Can you recall a moment you heard a story shared by a teacher, mentor, friend or co-worker that changed your life? Would your closest friends know what that story was and how it affected you? Why not?

10. It's tempting to reveal something shocking or amusing for comic effect, but limit your self-disclosure to a single positive anecdote that enhances your credibility. For instance, one speaker who was legally blind became a graphic designer. Perhaps you built your "SHE-shed" with your bare hands. Briefly write a relevant anecdote about yourself that would add to your credibility as an expert or an authority.

11. Is there a favorite quote from a famous person that you can use to make your point? Why does this quote speak to you? Use the internet to find inspiring quotes from presidents, inventors, artists, scientists, and poets.[29] Pick one you could use to begin a presentation with the quote as your opening line.

---

29 Brainy Quote is one of many websites that have an abundance of great sayings about many topics. https://www.brainyquote.com/

CHAPTER 10

Women Seen and Heard Speaker's Journal

When the Speaker is a Woman of Color

"I had two options. One was to remain silent and never to speak and then to be killed by the terrorists. The second option was to speak up for my rights and then die. And I chose the second one."
—Malala Yousafzai, Nobel Peace Prize Winner

The following questions are based on the prior chapter. If the audience is listening to a woman of color they may judge her on several levels: as an expert, as a person with a diverse viewpoint, as a token representative from a community of color. This further complicates the speaker's ability to be taken seriously as "the voice of authority."

1. If you are a woman of color or a woman with a particular cultural/ethnic background that often differs from your audience, whom do you imagine you represent when you speak in public? Do you represent your own opinions or those of your community? Are you preparing to represent your own unique expertise, the collective experience of your community, or the perspectives of your professional or business colleagues? Explain.

2. Do you feel pressure to represent something other than your own opinions when you speak up? If so, how does that make you feel? If not, explain why.

3. State a topic that you might address in the near future at a group meeting. How might your presentation vary depending on your listener's possible perspectives? These include people who share your background, work, and lifestyle. Would you matter to you as you framed your remarks? Explain why and how.

4. If you are listening to a woman speaker who is of a *different* ethnic, racial, or cultural group from yours, what comes to mind? Does that help or hinder your ability to listen to her key message points? Are you open- minded or aware of any biases that might inhibit paying full attention to her remarks?

5. Women play many roles in today's society. If you are a woman of color, how does the role you play affect your approach to planning a presentation or speaking in general? If you are not a woman of color, how would it affect your approach to speaking to women of color or women from different backgrounds?

6. If you are a woman of color and selected to speak at a planned meeting, conference or training program, have you clarified with the program planners why you think you were chosen as a speaker? For instance, did they specifically seek diverse speakers on the topic?

7. As a woman of color, have you ever felt as if you were chosen as a "token" representative to address a group? If so, did this affect the negotiation? If it did, how?

8. Think of a controversial topic you might address and the group you might speak to. What would your point be? State it in one sentence. What could you bring to this topic so that you have a fresh take?

9. Think of the controversial topics you might address. What assumptions might the listeners make about you having a bias based on your racial, cultural, ethnic group, age, gender, or sexual orientation? If your listeners might believe that you have a biased point of view that decreased your credibility, what could you say to reassure them and to change their minds?

10. If you are asked to speak on a controversial topic, how could you learn if your audience has a particular point of view before you prepare your remarks? This involves some detective work!

11. Why is it important that your references, expertise, and/or scholarship are accurate and current and conveyed in the introduction or in the program?

12. It's essential for a speaker to be sensitive to cultural differences. Issues like housing, childcare, employment, health care, and opportunities for advancement mean different things to different people. If you are not a person of color, how could you educate yourself to become more sensitive to and knowledgeable about the issues that different groups face?

13. What might you do to ensure that your topic relates to all people of all backgrounds?

14. What aspects of your culture would be interesting to people? (Consider art works, dress, photographs, foods, or music/musical instruments. Think about a particular topic that would be enhanced by these objects.)

15. What is a common myth or assumption about people of your background? How could your speaking or presentation style (or content) demonstrate that these myths and assumptions are untrue or biases?

16. Identify one group of people you might/should address but they have a very different background or point of view from yours. How could you find common ground?

17. Globalization forces us to work with people from different backgrounds and cultures. In order to solve common problems, we must appreciate one another's strengths, life experiences, and unique abilities. First, we must learn about our own cultural background and appreciate the various identities we have (rural or urban, parent, retired, large family, raised in a cold or warm climate, etc.). What are three interesting aspects of your culture and your identity that you could share with others? You might be more fascinating that you think!

Women Seen and Heard Speaker's Journal

Credibility as the Voice of Authority

"A leader takes people where they want to go. A great leader takes people where they don't necessarily want to go, but ought to be."
—Rosalynn Carter, First Lady and Advocate

1. Leaders mobilize people and get them to take action. When you influence people to do something, you are empowered. Your first task as a speaker is to gain the audience's trust as a credible authority. Where do you have the greatest self-confidence in your knowledge of how to do something or how to make something? Explain your source of self-confidence.

2. If credibility were based on academic knowledge, college degrees, or training certificates alone, how many fields of expertise could you name for yourself? (Consider the academic disciplines, businesses, professions, industries, occupations, and personal accomplishments. If your expertise comes from practical life experience, share that, too.)

3. What subjects are you able to speak about with expertise? List as many as you can.

4. Calculating your answers from the above questions, how many streams of formal learning (school) and life

experience (e.g., being a parent, traveler, "maker," or advocate) qualify you to speak about your chosen or favorite subject matter?

5. Women have many different ways of knowing things based on practical life experiences, travel, family life, and the duties required of women in typical families. What have you learned from life that you know to be true? For instance, my father was an immigrant and the first to attend college. His journey instilled in me a love of learning. List three or more of your "life lessons."

6. How many roles or perspectives have you occupied in your field of expertise? For instance, wisdom can come from years of working in your role or field, your experience as a leader, or mentoring younger people, etc. Describe what you have learned how to do from these various experiences?

7. You've likely been affected by political changes, environmental developments, fluctuations in the economy, technology, and work in our multi-cultural society and global economy. Give three examples of how your life has changed over the past one or two decades, as if you were speaking to a group.

8. You have both a unique perspective as an individual and a woman's perspective on today's emerging social issues and economic challenges. As a woman, what do you know that men wouldn't know or understand? Select any single hot issue of the day and express *your feelings* and *beliefs* as if speaking to a group about this issue.

9. MSNBC "Hardball" anchor Chris Matthews' tag line is "Tell me something I don't know." Do you have shocking information to share with your audience that will wake them up? Explain here! Give an example.

10. Share the "lessons learned" from your unique life experience. For example, you may have been a volunteer with a charity or campaign, a board member, an author of a published article, or traveled to an exotic place. Pick one or more and explain what you gained from any life experiences that transformed your life.

11. What are your core values—the principles you live by? Do you "walk the talk?" How do people know what your values are? How might your values be visible to groups you might be speaking to?

12. Politicians promise to lower taxes, make streets safer, and work with the opposition but they often don't deliver and aren't held accountable. Think about a promise that you made but weren't able to keep to your family, friends, groups, or in public meetings. How might you communicate progress to any of the above? Do you have any resources or networks who could help you make good on that promise, even belatedly?

CHAPTER 12

Women Seen and Heard Speaker's Journal

A Speaking Career

> "I've learned that people will forget what you said, people will forget what you did, but people will never forget how you made them feel."
> —Maya Angelou, Poet, Memoirist, and Civil Rights Activist

1. By the time you've spoken to many groups, you've received feedback. Are you able to accept the positive feedback you have received? What are the three most common positive comments you have heard about your presentations?

2. Have you ever considered developing your skills to the point that you could become a paid professional speaker? What would you have to give up, and what would you gain? List three pros and cons of life on "The Speaker Circuit."

3. There is IQ and there is EQ (or "Emotional Intelligence"). Without the ability to empathize with other people and "feel" for them, you can't connect. List three topics you feel connected to because you're not only a credible expert but because you care about the subject matter.

4. You have an interesting background and life/work experience to share. Let's assume you have honed your speaking skills and could deliver a dynamic motivational or inspirational presentation. Given an example of a spe-

cific audience or conference event that might hire you to be their keynote speaker.

5. A paid spokesperson works inside an organization representing their interests and communicating to various publics. Some well-known personalities lend their voice to a cause or charity. If you were to become a spokesperson for an organization, what type of organization would appeal to your values, interests, and knowledge?

6. Based on their professional delivery style, identify several popular female speakers you enjoy. They could be media personalities, actresses, comedians, political leaders, professors, journalists, scientists, CEOs, advocates/activists, or TED speakers. Explain what makes them positive role models for you.

7. Your listeners need to appreciate you, and the way you are introduced can do just that. How would you like to be introduced to the audience? What feelings would you like them to have before they actually hear you speak? [30]

8. Women are scrutinized more than men. You may not have robbed a bank but everyone has some sort of baggage at a certain age, and nobody's perfect. Media scrutiny is intense when a leader emerges. It's wise to be truthful about any setbacks, or issues you've struggled with. Let your audience know you are a genuine person with real challenges. Are there any aspects of your personal and professional life that might have to be resolved or addressed up front before you consider becoming a paid professional speaker? Where might you be vulnerable?

---

30 Our advice is to prepare your own ideal brief introduction and send it to the MC in advance, or take a copy of the introduction with you to your presentation. Leave nothing to chance!

9. Do you know people in business or professional groups who could open doors to speaking gigs? List five connections.

10. One group requires that any paid speaker is a published author. Another requires the speaker has worked in a global company in the executive suite. Consider a professional or business association of your choice and their meetings. What criteria would they use in selecting a paid professional speaker for their events? Then mention what you would have to do in order to meet their criteria and be chosen as their speaker.

11. Identify two individuals in your circle of friends or your network who could assist you in becoming a paid professional speaker. What questions would you ask them?

12. What is your "brand"? What makes you unique? Nike says "Just Do It!" and Virgin America started "Rock The Vote!" I'd say "Speaking To Inspire!" What could your bumper sticker or coffee cup say about you?

13. You have areas in which you're the expert. Are there topics you can blog about? Have you been published in conventional media? List 3 topics you know a great deal about and in which your perspective is unique.

14. Being visible on a conference panel where you can share your special expertise is a great way to gain confidence, expand your networks, and gain visibility. Are there panels you can volunteer for with particular organizations? List one organization that would benefit from hearing what you know to be true.

15. In today's world, you can become a celebrity overnight if an audience member or staffer posts your toast, presen-

tation, or keynote speech on YouTube. What would you like to change about yourself—if anything—to ensure you are seen at your best?

16. If you feel confident enough to build a professional speaking career, you'll need to produce a digital and a printed press kit. Gather together a recent digital photo, and information about your background, expertise, your favorite cause(s), titles of presentations you've given or can, testimonials, and any references. List your blog, published articles, interviews, and/or a book. Add testimonials from clients as you gain speaking engagements. Prepare a TO DO list here.

SECTION TWO

Speaker's Templates & Worksheets

INTRODUCTION TO USING THE
SPEAKER'S TEMPLATES

Why Did We Provide Templates?

Developing a flawless presentation begins with a strategy, or having a goal in mind. This requires preparation. But busy women will benefit from our nine templates, which are tools to help them focus fast and be most efficient with their time. These simple templates are provided as outlines to use to plan a briefing, presentation, or speech.

Templates are typically used to allow individuals to create their own personal layout for content; ours ensure that there is a logical flow as well as supportive evidence. This is particularly important when a woman pitches a big, complicated idea or inspires a reticent group with a call to action.

As professional speakers, we are often overwhelmed by the scale and scope of the information we can present. Organizing content can be a daunting task but it must be done. And the audience will appreciate being able to follow your logic as you present your key ideas. Sometimes less is more. Sometimes a picture is worth a thousand words.

Women Need To Transcend — Not Just Defy — Sex Role Expectations:

The templates we provide are foolproof strategies to gain credibility as "the voice of authority." The templates are based on women speaker's need to not only overcome but transcend the stereotypes in listeners' minds that can interfere with their ability to be taken seriously as leaders and thinkers. These attitudinal obstacles make it difficult for a woman to be seen and heard, and to have her content remembered. The best presentations a woman can make are strategically designed to combine logic and interesting facts relevant to a particular audience. Let's not forget the issue of personal relate-ability.

We saw how the "likability" quotient interfered with Hillary Clinton's electability. Women speakers must combine just the right equation of warmth and congeniality with stories and anecdotes, factual evidence and logic to drive home their Key Message Point. The more women prepare their presentations from this strategic perspective, the more likely it is that they can make an impact. And the positive feedback they'll get from their listeners will, in turn, build self-confidence.

Types of Presentations:

The templates reflect various types of presentations to include those intended to be informative, persuasive, humorous, or inspirational. To be clear, each type will reflect other purposes as well; for instance, the presentation to inform or persuade a group can have humor, and the inspirational presentation might have persuasive elements while containing lots of information organized to inspire the listeners. Each type of presentation is focused on one particular purpose, however, and people should leave knowing they were primarily informed, persuaded, entertained, or inspired.

Make the Templates Your Own:

You can elaborate on the templates provided and add in more Key Message Points as you finalize a presentation. Use the templates for practice and fun, or use any of them to produce a serious presentation to meet a deadline. Tear them out and copy them so you have more than one duplicate or use the E-book version that allows you to easily copy, paste, and re-cycle the templates.

We welcome feedback on how useful you find these templates. Communicate with us and offer feedback and suggestions through our website, www.WomenSeenandHeard.com.

TEMPLATE #1:
Producing an Informational Presentation

TO START: Write out a statement of your purpose and the ideal outcome of this presentation! Keep this in mind as you develop your ideas.

Introduction:

    A. Get the audience's attention by trying one of these ideas:

        Ripped from the headlines
        A shocking statistic!
        Great quote
        Stunning visual
        Joke or cartoon with a point to make
        Demonstration
        Rhetorical question

    B. Transition from the opener to the Key Message Point (E.g., "What does this mean?" or, "So here's the lesson.")

    C. State your Key Message Point (KMP) _____

Body:

    A. Develop your Key Message Point (KMP) by choosing one or more of these strategies:

        Explain further
        Give an example
        Tell a story
        Provide evidence
        Demonstrate
        Visualize your point; for example, show Before and After photos or a pie chart or bar graphs to show how a situation has changed over time.

B. Further Develop your KMP
    USE SAME STRATEGIES AS OUTLINED
    ABOVE IN "A"

C. Further Develop your KMP
    USE SAME STRATEGIES AS OUTLINED
    ABOVE IN "A"

Conclusion:

A. Summarize your KMP briefly in one sentence.

B. End with a great quote from a recognizable expert, state the lesson learned, ask a rhetorical questions, or state where "we" go from here.

TEMPLATE #2
Producing a Persuasive Presentation

TO START: Write out a statement of your purpose and the ideal outcome of this presentation! Keep this in mind as you develop your ideas.

Introduction:

A. Get their attention with a hook that immediately draws them in.

> Ripped from the headlines
> A shocking statistic!
> Great quote
> Stunning visual
> Joke or cartoon with a point to make
> Demonstration
> Rhetorical question

B. Suggest to the listeners why you are THE expert and know what you're talking about.[31]

C. Transition to your main point.

---

31 Listeners can be skeptical about the credibility of the speaker when it is a woman sharing a new or big idea or when she is addressing a controversial topic. Women who want to change minds and hearts have to quickly and consistently convey that they are ethical and trustworthy. Here are ways to convince the listeners that you have actual and unique knowledge/experience. Do so throughout your presentation:

1. State why you are the expert on this subject, and are trustworthy. Don't be modest or shy.
2. Explain why and how you can relate to the audience's needs, concerns, situation, and values.
3. Dramatize the problem! Clarify why action must be taken to do something as soon as possible!
4. Provide evidence, examples, show visuals, and provide anecdotes.
5. Reveal the weakness of the opposing point of view.
6. Tell a story that will appeal to the listeners' emotions to dramatize the urgency of a particular situation and why action must be taken soon.

D. State the problem or issue we face

Body:

A. Provide a few options that would address the issue, solve the problem, or meet the need:
   Option #1
   Option #2
   Option #3

B. Quote other experts who are respected by these listeners, but only those experts who would support point of view.

C. State preferred action and explain why it's the best idea.

D. Give several *benefits* of your proposal and who will be impacted (for the better) by when and how.

Conclusion:

A. Summarize the issue and the call to action in specific terms regarding what, when, who, and how.

B. Inspire the listeners with a great quote from a recognizable expert or ask a rhetorical question.

TEMPLATE #3
Producing an Inspirational Presentation

For instance, you might want to convince people that they can "succeed," however they define it.

TO START: Write out a statement of your purpose and the ideal outcome of this presentation! Keep this in mind as you develop your ideas. For instance, you might want to convince people that they can "succeed," however they define success.

Introduction:

A. Get the audience's attention.

B. Gain credibility as "the voice of authority," someone with integrity whom they can trust.

C. Provide surprising facts, statistics, and/or quotes from experts about your topic or about yourself.

Body:

A. Define "success" in personal terms and what's on your mind this particular day.

B. Focus on your point of view regarding what's at stake in the world today (or the particular situation that deeply affected you), and the action you took to advance yourself.

C. Take your story to a high level; e.g., clarify the choices you faced, the issues of "right vs. wrong," seeking the truth, what you learned from being the best you could be, profound issues of life vs. death, us vs. them, spirituality vs. material reality, and what matters most.

D. Convey the importance of *doing the right thing* in a complex dynamic world full of random events that we can't control. (Provide stories, anecdotes, and provide personal examples of how you or others overcame obstacles against all odds.)

E. Provide a moral message. Explain why it's important to have a moral compass.

F. What lessons did you learn from overcoming obstacles?

G. Tug at the heartstrings. Tell an emotional story that puts a human face on an issue or problem. Explain the consequences of not taking The High Road *in life in personal terms.*

H. Provide examples of a few specific objectives that the listeners can achieve in seeking high standards of living the "successful" life.

Conclusion:

A. Convey optimism with a "you can do this if I can" attitude!

B. Leave them with an inspirational quote and a specific call to action that they will remember.

TEMPLATE #4
Producing a Pitch Presentation for a New Product or Service

TO START: Write out a statement of your purpose and the ideal outcome of this presentation! Keep this in mind as you develop your ideas.

Introduction:

A. Get the listeners' attention. Shock them. Surprise them! Demonstrate the new product or service. Visualize the need with "before" and "after" statistics using a pie chart, photo or a cartoon!

B. Share *your credentials* as the expert who has the knowledge to understand what's at stake *and the big idea* to address the challenge (or need).

C. State your main point here in terms of the product or service you're pitching.[32]

Body:

A. Explain who will benefit from this new product or service.

B. Explain what will improve in terms of quality, reputation, innovation, morale, productivity, brand, diversification, etc.

C. List who is already behind this new product or service. (Include respected leaders, experts, scholars, researchers, etc.)

---

32 Many examples of different pitch statements:
- *We can become more competitive if we merge our businesses.*
- *We need to expand our R&D department. The inexpensive GIZMO I've invented will increase sales and revenue by twenty percent.*
- *We need to expand our company to include Asia satellites now.*
- *The company website had twenty thousand visitors and we can't keep up with the demand unless we hire more technical personnel immediately.*

D. Explain how this new product or service will not change what we love about our organization/present situation/company or agency.

E. Explain the consequences of not doing anything to meet an emerging need including the need to be more competitive.

F. Carpe Diem! Dramatize why we must act now, or else! What's at stake?

Conclusion:

A. Tell them what you want the listeners to do, the steps to take, with whom and by when.

B. End with an inspiring quote or a rhetorical question to support your call to action!

TEMPLATE #5
Producing a Persuasive Pitch to Propose Action

TO START: Write out a statement of your purpose and the ideal outcome of this presentation! Keep this in mind as you develop your ideas. Note that this template provides a "script" for you to follow, at least as you chart out the flow of how to present your own content.

Introduction:

A. Today's shocking headline reads...
(Always get the listener's attention with a hook, quote, rhetorical questions, or shocking statistics!)

B. Here's the situation we face. (Briefly explain the problem or need.)

C. I am an expert on this subject because... (Demonstrate why you're a credible expert with critical knowledge and history.)

D. I can relate to your situation/concerns/worries because... (Explain why you can empathize and are or were in their position in the past.)

E. We need to do something immediately to rectify this problem. Picture this... (Explain what might happen. Dramatize the consequences if no action is taken. Visualize the catastrophic consequences.)

Body:

A. Here are the options as I see them. (Lay them out as first, second, third actions to take, starting with the best one first.)

B. The best action to take is... (Explain your plan of attack in terms of the steps to take, who is involved, resources needed, logistics, and other specifics.)

C. Leaders in the field support my approach. (Select people who are reputable.)

D. Here's a story to illustrate how it would look or work. (Explain. Illustrate.)

E. Here are the 3 benefits of my approach to solving the problem. *(Explain: e.g., "First,....; second,....; third,....")*

Conclusion:

A. To summarize, I propose that we take action now by taking the first step, which is ....

B. As Marie Curie once said, "One never notices what has been done; one can only see what remains to be done." [33]

---

33 Quote an expert they respect. Ask a rhetorical question. Show a shocking image (again).

TEMPLATE #6
Delivering a Campaign Pitch³⁴

TO START: Write out a statement of your purpose and the ideal outcome of this presentation! Keep this in mind as you develop your ideas.

Introduction:

A. Get the audience's attention with a shocking headline, great quote, visual, or rhetorical question.

B. List the key issues facing voters who are or would be your constituents.

C. Indicate why you have the right stuff for addressing these issues:

> C1. State why you're running, including your passion for the opportunity to serve the public
>
> C2. Indicate that you have already demonstrated leadership capabilities and are ready for the job.

Body:

A. Explain your platform; state the issues you want to address or problems that need solutions.

B. Explain the impact of the issues on your local jurisdiction and community.

C. Share a personal anecdote to explain why you are affected by the pressing issues of the day.

D. Explain briefly and specifically how you will attack the top issues that this group cares about.

> D1. Emphasize your tenacity, true grit, and capacity to bring diverse people together.

---

34 See Appendix "Delivering a Campaign Pitch."

D2. Explain the benefits of voting for you,
given your life/work experiences and leadership roles.

E. Indicate persons who are supporting you, people whom
this group would respect.

F. Dramatize the need for a change. Say, "If nothing
changes, the consequences will be..."

Conclusion:

A. Ask for their support in very specific ways; for example,
ask them to donate to the campaign, help get press
coverage, organize house-parties, and get out the vote!

B. Leave them with something to think about! Use a
rhetorical question, a great quote, something ripped
from the headlines.

Template # 7
Producing a Humorous Presentation, with Examples

TO START: Write out a statement of your purpose and the ideal outcome of this presentation! Keep this in mind as you develop your ideas.

Sample Topic: "A Globetrotter's Strategies for Getting a Good Night's Sleep."

Introduction:

A. Get their attention with a rhetorical question;
Example: Have you ever woken up Grumpy?

B. *Transition—expand on that:*
Example: *Actually, in my case, no, but I have woken up Sleepy. I'm down to five or six hours a night. Really, getting a good night's sleep when you travel internationally is almost impossible. It's hard to know what country I'm in, much less what time it "really" is. But as CEO of TECH TOYS, I need to be on my toes, even in six-inch heels!*

C. *Main Point:* *Today I'm going to give you—as moms like me who travel for work—three strategies for getting a good night's sleep.*

Body:

These are a few examples only!

A. *Strategy #1:* *Stay in a hotel near an airport the night before a big trip. Don't even think of staying at home in your own bed. (Develop this idea.)*

B. *Strategy #2:* *If you must sleep at home, get into bed early with your most comfy PJ's and gorgeous meditative music, or provide your own amusing strategy.*

    C. Strategy #3: *Don't look at business materials after 6pm. Your mind will wrap around the deal.*

Conclusion:

    A. Restate your main point: *So I've given you three strategies for living without much sleep but keeping it together as an executive, as a mom, and as a partner.*

    B. Wrap it up! *Leave them smiling!*

EXAMPLE OF CLOSING QUOTE: The comedian Ray Romano once said that "Everyone should have kids. They are the greatest joy in the world. But they are also terrorists. You'll realize this as soon as they are born and they start using sleep deprivation to break you."

My kids prepared me to be successful in my present executive role multi-tasking from dawn to dusk. From parenting 3 young children to traveling the world for work, I can now say that sleep is highly overrated.

Template #8
Producing The "Small Wins" Briefing

TO START: Write out a statement of your purpose and the ideal outcome of this presentation! Keep this in mind as you develop your ideas.

Introduction:

A. GET THEIR ATTENTION (see prior templates)

B. EXPLAIN *The Small Win* you've achieved. State it clearly and mention who contributed.

Body:

A. COMPARE *The Small Win* to *The Big Win* you ultimately seek and show the value of progress being made.

B. INFORM the group regarding how you or your team achieved *The Small Win:*

B1. List the steps you took

B2. List the resources you needed

B3. List the obstacles you faced and describe how you overcame them

C. TELL STORIES /PROVIDE ANECDOTES about THE MEANING of *The Small Win* for your team and the larger organization/agency/institution/non-profit/ advocacy group

D. REPORT ON RESULTS of the small wins (financial, morale, diversification, press, etc.)

E. ALIGN *The Small Win* with THE BIG PICTURE, the future vision we seek.

E1. Show how this Small Win has BIG CON-SEQUENCES with a concrete example.

F. State how you think that the team/organization should REWARDED for *The Small Win*

Conclusion:

A. RESTATE YOUR MAIN POINT.

B. END WITH AN INSPIRATIONAL QUOTE OR A RHETORICAL QUESTION.

TEMPLATE #9
Delivering a Toast to the Bride and Groom

TO START: Write out a statement of your purpose and the ideal outcome of this presentation! Keep this in mind as you develop your ideas.

So often these are tasteless roasts instead of toasts. Show them how a toast (in a woman's voice) should be delivered!

Introduction:

A. Introduce yourself to the crowd.

B. Express how happy you are to share this day with everyone.

Body:

A. Indicate when you met the bride, groom, or both.

B. Indicate the depth of your friendship or history to include a brief example of something you shared (a trip, a school memory, being on the soccer team, or in a band together, or our mutual love of rock music).

C. Share history. Recall when the couple first met and indicate whether you had a part in introducing them.[35]

D. Tell a story about one or both. Give an example of a wonderful and positive trait or an incident that showed them at their best, portrays the bride and/or groom's uniqueness, and/or demonstrates an endearing quality.

E. Express your feelings. Give an example of *how you've been affected* by knowing one or both of them in a positive way.

---

35 Ask yourself: *When you heard they were a couple, what was your reaction? Was there an amusing incident they wouldn't mind you sharing? Did you realize how much they had in common or wonder if their different backgrounds and personalities would be challenging?*

F. Be sentimental. Express your desire that your friendship will continue throughout their lives.

G. Talk about what a great match they are. As a close friend or sibling of the bride or groom, chances are you'll honestly be able to speak on how they influence and complement each other. *Did you notice how they've changed each other for the better in terms of being good influences?*

Conclusion:

A. Wrap it up: As you near the end of the wedding toast, wish them both the best on their life journey together.

B. Raise your glass (and encourage guests to do the same) and extend a cheer to the happy couple and their future!

APPENDIX

Inspirational Speeches by Women

J.K. Rowling: "The Fringe Benefits of Failure, and the Importance of Imagination" (2008), https://news.harvard.edu/gazette/story/2008/06/text-of-j-k-rowling-speech/

Brené Brown: "The Power of Vulnerability" (2013), https://www.ted.com/talks/brene_brown_on_vulnerability/transcript?language=en

Ellen DeGeneres: Tulane University Commencement Speech (2009), https://www.c-span.org/video/?286414-1/tulane-university-commencement-address

Sheryl Sandberg: Harvard Business School Class Day Speech (2012), https://www.youtube.com/watch?v=iqm-XEqpayc

Elizabeth Gilbert: "Your Elusive Creative Genius" (2009) https://www.youtube.com/watch?v=86x-u-tz0MA

Vera Jones: "But the Blind Can Lead the Blind…" (2016), https://www.youtube.com/watch?v=faiPr_JqLgM

The World's Most Powerful Women, Speeches: https://www.youtube.com/watch?v=CtqBujiyfz8

Oprah's Commencement Speech at USC Annenberg School of Communication and Journalism, https://www.youtube.com/watch?v=DnKu46WGajo

Hillary Clinton's Commencement Speech at Wellesley, https://www.youtube.com/watch?v=aSwkS-GLVfE

Michelle Obama's Most Inspiring Speeches …., https://www.sheknows.com/entertainment/articles/1129553/michelle-obama-most-inspiring-speeches

10 Greatest All-Time Speeches by 10 inspirational women
https://www.marieclaire.co.uk/entertainment/people/
the-10-greatest-all-time-speeches-by-10-inspirational-
women-79732

Index of famous speeches by women is found here:

http://eloquentwoman.blogspot.com/p/the-eloquent-woman-
index-of-famous.html

Eleanor Roosevelt's Human Rights Speech, https://www.
youtube.com/watch?v=9yzakVOdh6k.html

Delivering a Campaign Pitch

First a heads up! A woman must give equal parts to empathy, qualifications, and her authority as a credible candidate. Use a "problem-solution" format and reinforce your unique brand throughout. And, along with establishing one's qualifications, "like-ability" matters because it is a key component of women's electability. A woman candidate must 1) talk about her accomplishments without modesty, 2) take credit for what she's done, can and will do, and 3) share a personal narrative.

Voters are also drawn to candidates who demonstrate passion and authenticity. Voters want to see a candidate who makes her values clear, who knows who she is, and what she stands for. Great political speakers have conveyed a positive attitude and optimism about the future that would see the county/State/country through the tough times. And, voters like it when a woman uses humor and presents herself in a way that is accessible and familiar. All this adds up to having a high score on the Trustworthiness Quotient (TQ)! Each woman can cultivate a winning personality that is unique to her as she gains experience on the campaign trail.

Producing A Humorous Presentation:
Being funny isn't feminine. Damn!

The template we provide on the Humorous Presentation needs some explaining.

> Men want someone who will appreciate their jokes, and women want someone who makes them laugh. The complementary nature of these desires is no accident. Researchers suspect humor has deep evolutionary roots—in 1872 Charles Darwin noticed chimpanzees giggling as they played—and many argue that the laws of natural selection can help explain the complex senses of humor we have today.[36]

People today are busy and distracted by the juggling act of everyday life that is especially common to many women who work, are parents, may engage in advocacy or activism, and may even be parenting parents. Women are often heard discussing how fragmented they feel to the point of madness.[37]

How to get listeners to pay attention is a key challenge for any speaker but professional speakers know that one way to do so is to get them to laugh. When people laugh they are relaxed and open. Once the audience is warmed up, the speaker can bridge to more serious topics.

---

36 "Fragmentia!" was the term coined by Lois Phillips in an article of the same name about the fragmentation of women's often conflicting roles. It is another way of describing what is commonly referred to as "women's juggling act." *Women in Education,* 1980.

37 The Humor Gap, Scientific American, Christie Nicholson on October 1, 2012

Alas, women will resist the idea of being funny for various reasons.

First, for most women, it's hard to tell a JOKE in the formal sense of the word. Sure, we might amuse our friends in our syncopated conversations but facing a crowd and getting the flow, timing, and punch line right is a whole other challenge. Joke telling is also tough for women given what men find funny and, let's face it, it's not *funny women*. For instance, one writer puts it this way:

> *"...there is something that you absolutely never hear from a male friend who is hymning his latest (female) love interest: "She's a real honey, has a life of her own . . . and, man, does she ever make 'em laugh." [38]*

Second, most humor is aggressive and preemptive. After all, "Male humor prefers the laugh to be at someone's expense, and understands that life is quite possibly a joke to begin with— and often a joke in extremely poor taste" while women prefer to take the high road, avoiding mockery and derision at someone else's expense. Think mother-in-law jokes, a type of humor that would never be used by a woman. Some of us actually love our mother-in-laws or are one.

Women amuse audiences by using humor as a tool, not a weapon. Women can surface and have a fresh take on the foibles of everyday life that are common to most women (and couples) today. True, women tend to overdo the self-deprecating humor but it works when it's necessary to make a point, as in "Have you ever panicked when you realized you left your baby on the bus?" or "The day's not complete unless I've lost my keys twice." As you describe the "Fragmentia" of women's lives, watch for the audience members nodding and rolling their eyes. Then, you can advance to a more serious issue, such as women's economic status.

38 Christopher Hitchens, "Why Women Aren't Funny," *Vanity Fair* January 1, 2007 https://www.vanityfair.com/culture/2007/01/hitchens200701

Also, the rise of identity politics has reinvigorated feminism and created a demand for points of view beyond those of white men. Arguably more important, however, is that media has caught up. Mass culture is in decline, and niche audiences are the goal. Social media has democratized the entertainment world by letting audiences directly express their approval with "likes" on FaceBook. YouTube and podcasts have made it possible to inexpensively create and disseminate work without a middleman.[39] Women who want to do standup comedy or become professional speakers known for their humor and wit can use social media to develop their own niche.

Let's get serious about humor. Being funny is empowering. When women do comedy, they are in charge. They know the reveal. They're a commanding presence. The comedic speaker dangles the punch line in front of the listeners. And they build up tension until the climax. How's that for a pun? Professionals explain further:

> *You're wielding the massive power of surprise. You're expressing your point of view in an especially potent way. Or, as Joan Rivers put it: "You're commanding them to listen to you."*[40]

We're happy to say women have role models. New talents have emerged to inspire the rest of us. From Dorothy Parker to Nora Ephron, we now have Fran Lebowitz, Ellen DeGeneres, Sandra Bernhard, Sara Silverman, Amy Poehler, Amy Schumer, Kristin Wilig, Kate McKinnon, Wanda Sykes, Margaret Cho, and Tina Fey, women who have cultivated the very unfeminine gift of being funny through self-deprecating humor and shtick. From belching in bed to bushes, they tell it like it is.[41]

---

39 "How To Produce A Podcast;" https://www.youtube.com/watch?v=j2C6Fx ZuvYU

40 "Why Comedy is Good for Girls and Women," http://www.goldcomedy. com/why-comedy-for-girls-and-women/

41 Ibid

Women today play conflicting roles. The demands upon women to be all things to all people are absolutely ridiculous. In everyday life, we women have often commiserated about that fact, bonding with girlfriends as we whine along with our wine. Together, everyone can laugh at life's absurdities and find common ground.

As women age, they often care less what people think and don't mince words. For instance, fashion icon Diane Von Furstenberg wrote that "Viagra is the worst thing that has happened to older couples, allowing 65 year old men to father children to 25 year old wives."[42] Really? Diane talks about senior sex in the most refreshing way that only women (or liberated men) can relate to.

Women comics are successful at the box office today because they describe the foibles of trying to navigate today's crazy world while keeping all the balls in the air. Comedians can deliver a one-liner that is sarcastic and unexpected, but their humor reminds us about the unfairness and inequities of life when the random assignment of bad luck lands on top of women's juggling act. Women wonder, "Why me?" Comedians answer, "Me, too."

19th century Shakespearean actor Edmund Kean is reputed to have said on his deathbed: "Dying is easy; Comedy is difficult."[43] The Humorous Presentation template we provide for you will help you become more amusing, if not downright funny. Are you ready to find the absurdity in everyday life that will engage your audience's attention before you pitch a new policy, product, service, or big idea?

---

42 "Diane von Furstenberg Is Not a Fan of Viagra," Opheli Garcia Lawler, STYLE, July 19, 2018 https://www.thecut.com/2018/07/diane-von-furstenberg-hates-viagra.html

43 Kean, Edmund. *Encyclopedia Britannica* (11th ed.). Cambridge University Press; https://en.wikipedia.org/wiki/Edmund_Kean